OMNIPRESENT
THE SACRED FEMININE BALANCE

CONTEMPLATIONS OF THE DIVINE ON EARTH

VIVIAN ANNALEE AVALON · JOSS BURNEL
DARA FOGEL · TAMARA LYNN RECTENWALD
JACQUELINE L. ROBINSON · BRITTANY N. SELLE
BETH SHEKINAH TERRENCE · MELISSA RAE THOMPSON

STARFIELD
PRESS
Oklahoma City, OK

OMNIPRESENT
THE SACRED FEMININE BALANCE

CONTEMPLATIONS OF THE DIVINE ON EARTH

VIVIAN ANNALEE AVALON · JOSS BURNEL
DARA FOGEL · TAMARA LYNN RECTENWALD
JACQUELINE L. ROBINSON · BRITTANY N. SELLE
BETH SHEKINAH TERRENCE · MELISSA RAE THOMPSON

TABLE of CONTENTS

VIVIAN ANNALEE AVALON

WHEN I WAS A child growing up, it never occurred to me that I could do or be anything I want.

Let me take this word "Feminine" and tell you what it means to me, as best I can in words, though being feminine—which I surely am—is something way bigger and more consuming than anything words can describe.

It is something you are. For me, it is being alive. I know I've been here in physical form many times, but I cannot imagine I have ever been here as a man! I just can't conceive of it. How would it be to be masculine? I used to be ever so grateful to God for letting me be born female. (Notice: "God LETTING me be…" "God, not GODDESS.") What I didn't know growing up, though, was that being female brings with it just as much responsibility, requires just as much strength and work as being male. I have to wonder if perhaps it was easier being male growing up in the sixties and seventies, simply because you would at least know what was expected of you.

I have to say I never thought of feminine as necessarily being divine. What is divine about it? Is it divine to be male? You can't have one without the other.

This brings the question "What is NOT divine?" Surely everything is divine, if one thing is. But feminine is so very raw, I've found — such hard work, and so exhausting. The nurturing can leave you weak, and if you are a nurturer, your job is never done. There will always be more nurturing to do, because the needs of all the others are very great.

It's not the giving of the nurture, though, that drains us so, but the caring so much about those in need of nurture. I have found that you will lose more sleep over those you are NOT able to help than those you can.

And we chant: Isis, Astarta, Diana, Hecate, Demeter, Kali, Innana, Eve, Mother Mary, Maya Angelou, Maid Mother and Crone, Amelia Earhart, Marie Laveau, The Three Graces, Mother Teresa, Sacagawea, Rosa Parks, Lilith, The Virgin

Queen, Billie Jean King, Anne Frank, Malala Yousafzai, Hattie McDaniel, Nefertiti...

Being Pagan, I am at times asked, "Who is your goddess?" My answer will always be "Me, I am my goddess—I am in fact THE goddess, Goddess of the Universe, there is no doubt about that. All the other goddesses are just fine, great in fact, and wonderful, of course, but I am THE goddess, and with a little help from my friends (many non-physical ones) I preside over my universe very effectively."

This, in my opinion, is how it must be, not just for me, but for all of us.

Are there gods in my world? Of course! Very powerful gods. But there is none more powerful than myself, and in my daily life of conquering and directing, I must remind myself of this fact often.

This is something that took many years for me to learn, and it's easy to slip into the old mode of days gone past—that false world of girls do it this way and boys do it that way and we always stay true to form. I may be a girlie-girl, but if a hole needs to be dug, I will find a shovel and sturdy shoes, and dig that hole... and plant that tree... and perhaps add some pansies around underneath, and may even cry a little when the pansies are destroyed by my dogs. My two great big male dogs. Remember, they dig holes too.

This world is divided into so many portions,

and labeled in so many different ways; how can one goddess keep up with it all? And does she want to?

Oh definitely.

Some goddesses do, and many gods do too.

This goddess likes to look at what's in front of her and love it. It's a pretty simple concept. Don't think for a minute that the rumbling of the mundane doesn't come into play daily. Things have to be done, there are places to be, and we must be on time. Yet time is an illusion. Time is an illusion. Time is an illusion.

And it really is.

It's not natural for me to be manlike. I'm not sure these days what manly is, but I would definitely recognize it if I saw it, and wouldn't criticize. Why shouldn't people—anyone—be who they naturally feel they are? It's not a man who abuses a woman, it's not a woman who succumbs to abuse. These are not defining things.

I believe it is individuals who decide who treats who a certain way regardless of sex.

In my day as a teen and young adult, there was this concept going around that men were not needed. Fatherless children were everywhere by design. Children only needed their mothers (or grandmothers), and it didn't matter if there was a father involved. Where is the balance in that?

Personally, I don't know what I would have done had it not been for my father. He was my rock, and when he was gone, there would never be another. Fathers are not disposable.

That being said, love itself is irreplaceable.

Can a father mother? Yes, I believe he can. Can a mother father? Yes, I believe she can. But it takes a certain something to fill these roles in child rearing. I believe it is something that comes naturally to some, but is very difficult to teach or learn.

As for myself, I am as feminine as they come, yet I have always felt I was a terrible mother. After having one child (fatherless, per se), I made sure I didn't have another. I made an even worse father than mother! So the concept that the child bearer is what sets us apart in importance — or in divinity — doesn't hold water in my book. I still have no desire to hold babies today. I have nothing against babies, but hand me a puppy any day, and I'll know what to do. A baby, not so much.

Now, the divine part.

How I love to watch as the eagle hunts to feed HIS young, and the male wolf protect HIS pack, keeping the cubs always safe. And that wonderful male human figure who dotes on his adorable little child, the little JuJu-bird — masterful to see! Male animals of the world divinely care for and nurture their young, right along with the goddesses of the world.

We must be who we are, regardless of who

we are, if we are to be happy, healthy, and enlightened. There will be boundaries and definitions, but there will also be melding. There will be acceptance and allowing. This is how it has to be, and will be, and already is.

In the focusing of the separateness, we find more opposition, so why put our focus there.

In the beginning, I said it never occurred to me that I could be anything I wanted when I grew up. This is true story. I thought I was supposed to be a certain way. I had dreams, but as a child didn't realize I could actually live them. I don't remember it ever being said to me, but I had the idea that all that stuff and the outcome of my life, would greatly depend upon a man. My household was governed and supported by a man. All major decisions were his. Most discipline came from him. It's just the way it was.

I always had the utmost respect for the male figure—and am not sorry that I did, but the female figure was not presented to me at that time as something strong and independent.

Today, I find myself being the strong and dependable one. I am the go-to person when those close to me are in trouble. I am the one who does what she says, and am always on time. Yet time is an illusion. Time is an illusion. Time is an illusion…

Who the hell is this goddess, anyway? Hercules (HER-cules)? Atlas (At-LASS)? Did you know Lassie is a boy, and Peter Pan is a girl?

Of course, there is the equality question. And to me, a question it is. What is equality? Is there ever equality with anything? Of course not.

I'm not talking equal pay, I'm talking EQUAL.

There are no two things that are the same. There are no two men or two women who are the exact same, with equal skill, equal knowledge, or equal education. Education comes in all forms of living. How can it be measured, really? IS an inch an inch? Have you ever seen an exact perfect inch? Was it angry?

Oh, that's another topic.

Sorry.

The point is, so much relies upon perception. Who thinks what, and who is judging? What kind of mood were they in that day? If they're a woman, what time of the month is it? How many times has that time of the month influenced the way you act, react, judge, and feel? It always influencing, I know—and naturally so. How many pre-teen girls and teenagers are being fed mind-altering drugs for going through what has been perfectly natural since the beginning of humanity? Why can't we be naturally female, naturally feminine, naturally human, and it be okay?

Oh, yes, women are taking over the world. Everyone knows that. There are more females than males in universities today. The male figure is somewhat fading in our society. We kind of like to make fun of them, these male creatures who tend to think with something other than their brain. Advertisers target the female, the money spender, and the moneymaker!

But equal pay? True power in the workplace? Maybe we're not there quite yet.

Women of the world unite, build up their strengths, shout out and sing loud in harmony and disharmony—they will be heard! Girls of the world, who are you? What are your dreams? You are strong, you are smart, you are beautiful! As it's quoted, "You is kind. You is smart. You is important." Don't give up!

Baby making is no longer our most important role. Where does that leave the babies who are made? Are babies playing second fiddle to careers? As long as babies are being made, perhaps it's best we do some prioritizing. We want to teach our girls and boys well, but mothers, isn't it always best that we ourselves be the teachers? Something is bound to be lost in translation if we leave the teaching up to our respective daycare workers and preschool teachers. Of course, we strive to set a good example, but what example are we setting if we leave our babes in pursuit of careers and money? But we have to work, we have to provide, we have to survive, yes? There will be enough time to raise our children, we will make time in the evenings, on the weekend, whenever. But time is an illusion. Time is an illusion. Time is an illusion…

Where's dad? Therein lies the answer, does it not? If mother and father—female role model and male role model—join forces, how much more powerful is the teaching, the example setting, the life lessons, the time?

Enough about teaching and such.

Who are we, women? We used to be called the weaker sex. They were wrong. We are strong, extremely strong. We At-LASSES carry the world on our shoulders, and keep going and going and going. We do it all. We conquer every profession, sport, climb every mountain, and follow every rainbow. We cannot be crushed. We alone hold the power to our successes or failures, and we will always carry on.

Me? At times I am Marilyn Monroe, at times I am Queen of the Nile! At times I am Norma Jean. At times I am a kitten, but at times I am a lion. I want to love what's in front of me. I want to love where I live, what I do, and who I am. I do not want to be beholden to any man—or woman for that matter—for anything. I want only myself to answer to for my choices.

I don't need permission or forgiveness. I am Mother Nature, I am Goddess, I am Divine.

VIVIAN ANNALEE AVALON can be found online at **MyLadyoftheLake.wordpress.com** and on Facebook at **Facebook.com/Vivian.Noah**

She loves to hear from others, and can be emailed at **ladyofthelake.avalon@gmail.com**

JOSS BURNEL

I CAME LATE TO the table to participate in the banquet laid out before us. Unsure of my invitation, unwilling to participate in something I didn't quite fully understand, I stood outside the banquet hall looking in, listening, and waiting to discover if this was my place of belonging.

And then She smiled at me. She smiled at me in the flight of the dragonfly and the rising of the moon, and I fell deeply, madly in love with the Divine Feminine.

Since that moment, I have read and I have journaled. I have taken courses, and I have been in meditative thought. Most of all, I have allowed myself to sink deep into my body, to plumb the depths of my own heart.

Our world has been in a sad place for far too long—a place where the Divine Feminine was taught to be silent, to hide and be ashamed. A place where Patriarchy took command of the Divine Masculine, and emasculated Him.

We have woken up, and we are reclaiming what was known of old: that for our world to heal, we need more. More than what we have been taught for hundreds of years, more than we have been allowed to be. We have only to look at the universe, at the natural world, at this very planet to know that all exists in balance and beauty, and so must we.

The way of either/or, of black and white, of measuring our value by our possessions, of turning sensuality into depravity, of valuing the mind over the heart, has brought us nothing but destruction and fear.

Enough.

That way needs to be abandoned, and we must—we ARE—spiraling back inward, where beauty and grace reside, where the Divine Feminine and the Divine Masculine lie down together and love one another on the soft green grass.

This is what my heart longs for; this is what I know.

And the knowing comes from being with Her, from spending time alone in Her presence, and allowing to unfold within me the memory of our connection, of my connection to the Divine Feminine in all her glory.

If you would know her
you must lower your shields
you must allow your heart
to breath in the perfume
of the sweet pea in late afternoon

If you would know her
you only need to watch
the tide move out
towards the vast expanse
that knows no borders

If you struggle to understand her,
be present
to the music of the whippoorwill
feel the sound of her voice
as she rides in on thunder
and asks that you tremble
at her power

I am gentle and kind
She says
as She holds out her hand
to the newborn deer
and lays a kiss upon its head

I am the wind that blows
the rose that blooms

the sap running through the tree
as it rises up and confounds
all your silly laws of gravity

I am that moment
of orgasm
when you lose all thought
all knowing
that moment when time
stands still and you
are able to touch the
hand of God

Your planet, your home
knows me well
and feels me move
in earthquake and trembling leaf
in silent dawn
and thunderous seas

I am all of creation
I am birthing
and dying and I am
every breath you take
there is nothing that does not
contain me —
even you

I invite you to come
yes, to come
to allow your body

that sweet release
that rising out of your body
and into the stars
feel me there
know me there

When you sit and watch
the sunrise
when you stretch out your arms
and dance under the moonlight
when you curl up under the stars
I am there
in all that is

I am your heart beating
with fear
your breath catching
in awe
your body reverberating
with anger
at the destruction you
have wrought

Where have you been
you ask
where are you
cries your heart
Where have YOU been
is her shout
Where have you been?

Come now
let us join together
let us fill the space
of emptiness
that has grown between us
with love
with laughter
with labour
to repair all that
was broken
all that has been
destroyed
let us rebuild
nay, let us recreate
a world where we
walk together
male and female
in harmony
in Divinity
in grace.

This is how I see the Divine Feminine in all her glory and power. It is time for us to set aside our polarized thinking, our separating ourselves from one another, from the wolf and the raven. We are a part of this amazing planet, this vast universe of light and magic. We belong together, and we must work together to birth again the old ways — the old ways of walking on the earth with respect and harmony, the old ways of holding sacred our bodies, our sexuality, our very breath.

We are so much more than we have allowed ourselves to be these past few centuries.

The planet is Her voice, and we are hearing her screams of agony in tsunamis, in wild fires, in earth tremors, and in a vast climate change that is impacting our lives — our very structured narrow lives. She calls us to expand our vision, widen our horizons and see, and know, that we matter more than we have allowed ourselves to imagine. We matter. What we do, what we say, who we are makes a difference. We need to reclaim our true nature as fellow caretakers of the land, and to walk upon it with awareness that we impact all of creation.

We have been out of balance for too long. The Divine Feminine is reaching out a hand of salvation, and longs for us to sink in to our greatness and love one another once again.

I will see you on the wind
And hear your voice on the morning dew
I will know your presence
as I cleanse my body
And walk with you upon the water
I will make love to you
upon the fresh green moss
And sense you in the beating of my heart
I will be present to the unfolding of the rose
And be the crow that calls your name
The veil between us has parted

*And we are present and known
as never before.
All that has come before is done.
And now magic awaits.*

————————ɪ(✳)ɪ————————

JOSS BURNEL has been writing poetry as a means of expressing wisdom and grace for 35 years. A Certified Holistic Coach, her spirituality and mystical approach to life has risen from a heart hungry to know more, to see deeper, to be aware of the world through the eyes of sacredness.

From years as a pastor's wife, to homeschooling, to teaching French, to administrative support, to taking a year off on pilgrimage through France, her path has led her deeper and deeper into an awareness of God's presence — a God she knows personally and loves with her whole heart.

The author of *If God Was A Woman*, Joss believes patriarchy and organized religion has done us the disservice of painting a picture of God as wholly male and dominant. She invites you to enter the labyrinth with her, and consider that God is way more than you ever imagined.

DARA FOGEL

Reclaiming the Crone

"**W**HAT THEY DON'T TELL you is that you go from being the most important person in the whole world to being nobody—absolutely nobody!"

The old woman in the motorized chair at the grocery store volunteered her views of the changing roles of womanhood, after I had helped her get some out-of-reach cookies.

"Nobody sees you if you're not young and sexy."

A friend at lunch told me that she dreaded and feared menopause, with its anticipated hot flashes and emotional swirliness.

The menopausal and post-menopausal woman has become a tired cliché, worthy of multiple cartoons and Facebook memes. Everyone hears about the hot flashes, mood swings, and other hormone-driven crankiness. But now that I have crossed that hated threshold myself, I find that it both is and is not what our culture claims. Very few people these days seem to be talking about the power of the Crone—the archetype of the wise older woman—the healer, the counselor, the seer.

Most older women images in the mainstream media are commonly portrayed as eccentric ("crazy cat ladies" and "purple ladies" come immediately to mind) or controlling bitches (evil mother-in-laws and wicked witches) or comfortably benign (like Grandma or the little old lady you help with her trash). But all of these are cultural stereotypes that belie the true spiritual transformation that women undertake when the majority of their energies are no longer focused on reproduction, just like the sweet little old lady I met at the grocery store revealed a depth of legitimate outrage at how culture has discarded her.

When I was younger, I spent an absurd amount of time trying to conform to my society's standards of what a Woman was supposed to be. I made sure my body and appearance was sufficiently appealing to standards set not by me, nor taking my uniqueness into consideration. I adopted these unconsciously, nonetheless, internalizing values designed to sell the products of fashion and body care merchandisers. Even when I thought I was rebelling, I was still controlled by those external standards, such as when I decided to quit shaving my legs, but was too ashamed to wear shorts or skirts. Everything revolved around being perceived as sexually desirable, whether I intended to follow through with it or not—the perception of sexual viability was the underlying bottom line.

Our culture focuses almost exclusively on the Maiden and the Mother archetypes of womanhood, mostly ignoring the third phase of life: the Crone—the holder of ancient knowledge.

When thinking about the Divine Feminine, it is very difficult to draw distinctions between religion, politics, and culture. Patriarchy has devalued and buried Women's Mysteries so thoroughly and for so long that reclaiming the ancient feminine archetypes has become largely an archeological endeavor.

Patriarchy has more or less preserved those aspects of the Divine Feminine that served their purposes: the Maiden and the Mother. But the Crone was reviled and denigrated for so many centuries that by the twentieth century, crones were feared and rejected, resulting in the devaluation of older women to the status of essential non-being.

In the last two decades, we have begun to see a re-emergence of the archetype of Crone, as Baby Boomers reached menopause and beyond. But in many cases, the older women serving as role models have sacrificed much of the Divine Feminine within them in order to succeed in the patriarchy. We see a few of these women, who have managed to rise to the top in business and politics. But in many cases, these women have become powerful by playing by patriarchy's rules, compromising their innate Yin energies, making themselves more Yang to fit into the "Good Ol' Boys Club." While it is good to see at least some women in high office, the policies and agendas they promote from those offices are more often than not disassociated from both the knowledge of the ancients and the wisdom of Gaia.

According to Jungian psychologist Marie Louise von Franz, when a quality of our nature is denied dignity or consciousness, it goes "rancid." (Johnson, 1990) In other words, when our natural gifts, talents, and being are not included or are degraded, then they become a part of our "shadow," becoming twisted and fearful, often leading to our own downfall. This is what has happened in our youth-oriented culture—the later phases of femaleness are ignored and neglected at precisely the time that women begin to understand who they are and what they believe and why.

In return, older women succumb to the negative status and patronizing stereotypes assigned to "non-breeders" in our culture. Although older women are to be found everywhere in our cities and towns, menopausal and post-menopausal women are often merely tolerated, but not exactly welcomed in many public spheres.

The older woman who isn't "trying" to be a sex object is viewed as "letting herself go," as if the appearance of sexual viability is the optimal value for all adult women, and those who do not conform are judged and shamed harshly.

And yet, when a woman ceases to prioritize sexual enhancement, or her children grow and leave the nest, are precisely the time when more of her vital energies are available to connect with her own innate wisdom, to pass on her knowledge and skills, to mentor the next generation.

For it is only when the demands of others relent does a woman have the opportunity to become more authentically herself. But in a culture where it is taboo for women to value their own personal development on par with that of their children, far too many older women end up like the woman at the grocery store—feeling abandoned, useless, and bitter.

But it need not be that way, for the third part of a woman's life is every bit as potent as the previous two. The Crone phase of life is a remarkable time, when a woman has enough life experiences under her belt to see the recurring cycles and patterns in life, as well as having fewer distractions pulling her away. But when women are not taught about that aspect of the Divine Feminine, they can feel discarded rather than empowered, lost rather than soul-directed.

For most of their lives, women are conditioned to look outside of themselves for validation, to place the needs of others before their own. It is no wonder that they lose touch with their own inner values, when they believe that they must meet the expectations of others. And when those others no longer require them, these women seem to be cut adrift, left without a center to orbit.

Luckily, we are beginning to see a few older women rising to model Crone dynamics in the mainstream media, such as Jane Fonda and Lily Tomlin's new Netflix series, *Grace and Frankie*, about a couple of septogenerians stuck together when their husbands come out of the closet. The comic drama deals with some of the feelings of abandonment and loss of purpose experienced by many post-menopausal women, as well as explores the potential for re-connection with our deepest selves, once all the cultural veils are stripped away. But this new show is an exception to the trend of mainstream media, which tends to focus on younger audiences.

As the U.S. population ages, more and more women are subjected to this dearth of positive role models for women past the age of childbearing, undermining self-worth and ambition. It is the wisdom of the elder woman who looks beyond immediate survival, to consider the needs of future generations. But in our culture of immediate gratification, the well-being of future generations has no meaning to the bottom line.

Older women are the torch-bearers of tradition, the midwives of both transformations of birth and death. Yet patriarchy has usurped these roles, leaving modern generations of elder women without the foundation, esteem, and social contribution that once made for strong and effective crone leaders. This usurpation of the final phase of the Divine Feminine has left the world dangerously unbalanced, as masculine values like consumerism and conflict continue to prevail over integration and wholeness.

"Juicy Croning" is still a radical idea whose time is yet to come, yet we desperately need to access the innate wisdom of the waning phase of the Divine Feminine, to include and welcome the stabilizing impact of the Crone if we are to find balance in our culture, our environment and our spirits.

————————ɪ(✳)ɪ————————

DARA FOGEL, Ph.D. is a philosopher, author, and educator. She holds a doctorate in Philosophy from the University of Oklahoma and has taught philosophy, religious studies, and humanities at several universities and colleges in the Southwest.

Fogel underwent a series of spiritual awakenings following a life-threatening illness in 1990. She has published four books inspired by her experiences, including her bestselling steampunk conspiracy series, the *GrailChase Chronicles*, and one non-fiction.

A confirmed geek, she bridges the gaps between popular culture, cutting edge sciences, mysticism, philosophy, and dramaturgy, to bring a deeper perspective of self-knowledge and ancient wisdom to new audiences. Her essay, *Life in the Holodeck*, will be included in Blackwell's upcoming volume, *The Ultimate Star Trek and Philosophy*, due out spring 2016.

Although there are no new ideas under the sun, there are infinite combinations and understandings of the recurring cycles and patterns of the underlying oneness of life.

TAMARA LYNN RECTENWALD

THE DIVINE FEMININE, THE essence that is inborn in the womb, is never nature versus nurture. It is always a nurturing nature that she radiates.

She is the vessel of creation, indulging in conception and the mystery of birthing a Soul into human form—a Divine Love, nourishing with her receptiveness, patience, and quietude, all while allowing her light to continue to shine and nourish the divine creation within. She allows life to flow through her.

She gives effortlessly, knowing Divine flow will return to her.

She accomplishes all through the heart of compassion, and an understanding that only she knows.

She loves for no reason, and exudes this radiance from the Heart, sharing it with all. She is whole, content, and complete at her core, which allows her to move herself with an unshakable confidence that everything that happens is part of a divine plan.

She is the healer that which, through her unwavering love, guides us back to our North, where all is brought into alignment, creating wholeness and balance.

She will nudge you continuously, helping you to remember why you are here, where you came from, and who you are at your very core.

She holds space silently in her heart for others to grow, heal, and expand. She is that comfort we return to, knowing we are home and safe.

She is that universal desire waiting patiently for Awakening, Love, Peace, Health, and Abundance for all to permeate and heal our Planet.

She allows her darkness to permeate her being, knowing that from darkness, a rebirth must occur in order for her to rise up and claim her divinity.

She fills herself first, allowing it to spill over to all.

She is the guard to her inner temple, her Heart that allows love to blanket all she touches.

She is the observer, keeping an eye out to see

that all flows harmoniously, reminding us of our oneness, not of being separate.

She embraces her darkness, knowing she will find her power and rise to remember her true authentic self.

She is the nourishment that feeds our soul, as fed and nurtured in the womb. She is the Divine Feminine, the goddess within.

She is You.

Rise, remember and embrace.

———————◦◀❋▶◦———————

TAMARA LYNN RECTENWALD became a Certified Crystal Healer in 2012 through the Hibiscus Moon Crystal Academy. Through her travels, love, and knowledge of crystals, she created *Pura Vida Crystals*. Tamara loves to share not only their beauty, but their healing frequencies as well.

Having studied the chakra system for over 10 years, Tamara received her certification as a Kundalini Reiki Master/Teacher in 2013. She loves all things energy, and also has other certifications in alternative healing modalities.

Tamara is currently involved in her yoga teacher training journey, being certified through YogaFit, completing Level I, along with her Seniors and Children certifications.

Nothing makes Tamara more happy than

guiding those to begin their healing journey and remember who they truly are.

Tamara can be found at her website **PuraVidaCrystals.com**, and reached on Facebook at **Facebook.com/PuraVidaCrystals** or Twitter at **@CrystalPuraVida**. She also invites you to her blog at **puravidacrystals.wordpress.com**

JACQUELINE L. ROBINSON

I FIRST ENCOUNTERED AND learned of her presence — the Divine Feminine — in the winter of 2004. Having grown up in a religious and patriarchal family, she'd been foreign, invisible, and absent to me for most of my life. Then I read *The DaVinci Code*, and my world changed instantly. I'd never known of the Sacred Feminine, and yet as I read of her existence throughout history, I could easily sense her with me in present time. A hunger was born in me, and I couldn't get enough of her as a faint, ancient reflection of myself began to whisper from the mists.

It's part of her magic — whispering into our hearts reminders of a code of truth only we are equipped to decipher. Each of us bears our own code. Not one aspect of the Divine Feminine holds the same DNA as another. We carry unique expressions and visions of the Sacred Feminine. It is both our legacy and our purpose to embrace all that she is within us.

My life would never be the same after 2004. In the eleven years since I first felt her energy in my own body, I have more and more awakened into my own imprint of her presence—sensual, fiery, filled with feeling and a need to express it, longing for intimacy on every level, hungry to feed on the pleasures of her abundant gifts and joys in this life, aching to sink into the darkness of her womb and find solace, comfort, and grace. She has consumed me, and I—over and over again—give myself to her.

Engage Your Passions: The Fiery Feminine

The Fiery Feminine is so much the crux of who I am, of all I have witnessed, carried, and stirred in this life of mine. From the time I was a child, I was innately aware of my own sensuality.

Consider the term sensuality and all it arouses. We're mostly familiar with the patriarchal characterization of it: sinful, evil, temptation, wicked, etc. This is very much the way so many of us have been programmed to veer away from the essence of who we are. For if we are unable to tune in to our own truth through the electricity of our senses, we become programmable, trainable — tamed.

Sensuality is in its purest form the experience of life through the senses. Let us explore how that comes into being through our everyday lives, with the full intent of washing away that which lives within us and is yet untrue, and of calling awake the receptors of our own sensing, our own intimate and holy knowing. Come with me now, giving yourself permission to feel and experience only what comes through your body as we move together. Imagine yourself in the moment, eyes closed or awake, body fully relaxed, senses open to whatever may arise in you.

Bring to your awareness the taste of something you love — be it sweet or savory, deeply refreshing and inviting to your own distinct palate. Remember what it is to kiss with your own lips the mouth, the heart, the forehead, belly, thighs, and wrists of those you love. Feel into the experience of being loved, of laughter and joy, of tears and heartache — sinking deeply into the sensation of every rise and fall present now in your own emotional rhythm. Whisper words from your lips you've always wanted to utter but perhaps never dared — even if only to yourself. Open your eyes to what is before you, pausing, taking the space of a breath to really see beyond what is obvious, gazing deeper into the beauty you have chosen to surround yourself with as who you are, in your home, with your partner, through your children, in the experience of Nature that encompasses you. Listen with your ears to the birdsong calling you: the gentle or perhaps percussion-rich harmony of music moving your body and softening your edges. This, Loves, THIS is the art of your own sensuality.

We have for too long turned ourselves off in favor of being "good," of doing the right thing, honoring this rule or that, and not upsetting the status quo prevalent in ourselves and reflected through others. We have quieted our own voice in favor of another's, chosen to taste life from their buffet rather than frequent our own, walking in shoes of those who appear to know more than we do.

But we are waking up fully now—some of us over the course of years, a bit at a time, and others seemingly in an instant. It matters not how you have come to this point, to reading this book, and moving deeper into the heart of your own soul, for we each experience the inhale and coupled exhale of who we are as we journey to the depths. We each have moments when the fog is so thick we can barely see our own flesh; in another instant we stand tall in our being, knowing fully who we are with the most precise vision.

The Divine Feminine has come alive with a fervor, with a grace and elegance. She is dancing to the rhythm of love. Not the kind of love that is light and sprightly—the kind of love that drives us into a fierce wave of passion and ecstasy and as certainly drops us into a pit of messy despair.

She is all that, and so much more.

We have shut her down—from the inside out as well as the outside in—with an effort to shield ourselves from the raw intensity of who we are, of all we feel. Our very own survival instinct has broken down the lines of communication between our sacred center and the obedient servant of "rightness" we have become molded into through years and lifetimes of silencing.

This is our time now, our time to dig deep into the recesses of our knowing, of our presence, of our true essence. That is where we find the purity of our own "rightness." There is no other who can know it as truly as we do. No other who holds the keys to our unique Divine Feminine expression.

Let's Talk About Sex

For much of my life, I confused my own sexuality with Divine Feminine sensuality. The visible shift began in 2009 as I asked one of my teachers why I would feel so turned on in my body when we were talking about the Sacred Feminine, as I was feeling connected and merging with "God." His answer to me left me empty and hungry for something more, although I now have some understanding of why he simply said, "Oh, my dear, it would take me hours to explain that," with a little pat on my knee.

I was frustrated for sure. Even more I turned on myself, believing something must be wrong with me. As far back as three years old, I remember loving boys, playing under the bed with my little friend as we showed each other our "private parts." Even then we felt the need to hide it, although we couldn't have known why.

There is a very distinct memory I have of being five, wearing my favorite kindergarten black dress with white polka dots, and lying on the grass in my friend's yard. He was a few years older than me. I remember him lifting my dress and doing something to my body, telling me this is how they make babies.

It's not an unusual experience, right? So many of us have one of these stories in our history, coupled with feelings of having been violated. It didn't feel that way to me—violated. It felt normal, fine, no big deal. I wasn't mad or hurt, nor did those feelings ever come. I feel like we were kids, acting out what we saw, heard, or understood from grown ups, and perhaps even from our own instinctual knowing. We weren't abusing or violating each other. We were being kids, playing out the moments of life. And still, we were in the woods, somehow sensing a need to hide it, to lock away our own curiosity and innocence in a world where anything "sexual" is wrong outside of rigid rules—and certainly ALWAYS wrong for children who don't understand. Only, we weren't being sexual. Not to us. We were being ourselves, exploring, pretending, feeling our way through something we related to on some level.

I want to pause a moment here and say in no way am I discrediting any other person's experience or resulting feelings. These experiences are my own, part of my story, my sensations and energies. My intention in sharing these pieces is to provide another lens through which to see ourselves, to connect to the Divine Feminine and her patterns and presence throughout the entirety of our lives, and indeed all of time. For me to see the sexual engagements throughout my life, and to witness my own response to them has been immensely powerful in understanding who I am, releasing guilt and shame, and embracing the supposed "not so pretty" part of me. They are all part of Her as Me—every single piece of my life.

My love of the masculine and desire to see,

feel, and touch the fire of our coming together continued throughout my childhood and adult years. I was in trouble in first grade for kissing a boy, and couldn't watch *Little House on the Prairie* for a week. This was huge, as we were fundamental Baptists and television was mostly off limits. As much as I loved Laura Ingalls, kissing felt much more exciting to me.

There was spin the bottle in the woods in fifth grade, secret kissing again in sixth grade, and books with sex scenes in them in seventh grade — and on it went. Mind you, my entire education was through private Christian schooling, so these offenses were even more "dirty," and as I grew older became attached to words like slut, whore, and cheap. The emotions these words evoked in me were confusion, devastation, shame, embarrassment, rejection of who I am and of what felt natural in me.

As the years went on, I more and more believed something must be wrong with me. I was often thinking about boys and kissing, touching, feeling. Nothing really mattered more. And it wasn't just the sex — it was the connection, the union, the fire, the love, the intensity and passion I craved. For me, being sexual with someone else was my doorway into ecstasy, and in many ways, into myself. I knew it, but I had no sense of what that truly meant until these last few years.

The more I have let go of what anyone else thinks or feels, the more I have given myself permission to feel sexual, to express it, to share it with others who either relate and/or have the ability to accept me as I am, the more unleashed my patriarchal binds have become. The more I stop feeling wrong, or bad, or ashamed, the less I hide my true self.

What I've learned in this span of time these last couple of years especially is that for me, sexuality is a very big part of who I am. But it's not about the sex. It's about breaking down the barriers to my own sensual receptors, surrendering completely into the moment of what I FEEL rather than what my mind dictates as right or wrong.

Rebel Heart:
"Naughty" and "Taboo"

I've grown to recognize another element of the Divine Feminine energy that runs through my being—rebellion. Rebellion as an act of rejecting anything that isn't mine, that doesn't feel true to my own internal soul code. Part of what turns me on energetically is the fire of blazing my own path, refusing to conform to what someone else's standards are for me, and to my own programmed and inherited perception of "black and white."

Rebellion can go one of two ways. It can serve as a holy tool of change, or it can take on a life of its own and leave us rebelling for the sake of it, simply because we aren't grounded in who we are or what we believe.

My own way of connecting with life—through engaging my senses completely—was natural in me as a child. As the years went by and the organic societal and religious expectations were brought into my awareness, the natural in me began to shift into something ugly, bad, dirty. It was in that space of time that a full-on rebellion against myself began. In my energetic makeup, I am a rebel. I have a very pure need to break the rules, to pursue that which is taboo or hidden, to feel the exhilaration of the moment I am "outside the box."

I understand now that my own personal Divine Feminine rebellion is to continually set aside that which is not mine. Sex is not dirty. My desire to sample every pleasure and delicacy this life has to offer is not wrong. We have for too long labeled who we are with such words as addict, indulgent, out of balance, etc. We have depended upon someone else's feelings, ideas, beliefs, and truths to define our own feelings and natural energetic flow. The key to our own liberation lies in our ability to FEEL what is pulsing in our own blood and give honor to our own intimate truth.

Everything is Right:
The Dark Feminine

Even in our darkest moments, what if we understood "everything is right," right now, in this very minute? How might our response, our experience, our lives be different?

I am a firm believer that every choice we make in life is ours and is in reality for our own good, even when it feels the opposite, even when no one else gets it, even when we are swimming in the deepest despair we have ever felt or are lying sick on the couch for weeks. Every part of our life is right.

I've recently come through a space of illness. It took me by surprise, although I had known my thyroid wasn't functioning in the way my body needs. The challenge for me in this was coming from a time of feeling exceptional, of not needing any care or treatment for the long term illness, very much believing and celebrating that I had healed my fifth chakra. My thyroid had stopped producing too much hormone, and all the work I'd done to liberate my voice, to speak my truth and allow myself all manner of expression had shifted the course of my health. But it was time for the next shift to run its cycle.

When blood tests showed my thyroid had turned in the opposite direction and was no longer producing enough hormone for my body, I committed to natural supplements and healing: no hormone treatment for me. "That's medical, they never get it right, it's synthetic and I'm not doing it." (Rebel in motion). I chose to take a natural route. And it worked—for a while, until I began to sense something really wasn't right and felt strongly in my being it was time to go to a doctor.

That decision did not come easy.

I wrestled with myself and everything I had believed until that point. To go to a medical doctor felt like self-betrayal. There were conversations with my husband, with others who offered their own intuitive insights. I tried several options that had proven effective in my life in other places and ways, but nothing worked.

The decision to call a specialist was no small thing. On my own spiritual path, the act of surrender has played a very big role. It seemed as though the surrender would typically be to exploring natural healing options. In my case, the biggest act of surrender I've made in the twenty years of this illness has been to call the doctor this time. I cried over it. A lot.

What I learned as I laid on the couch already unwell from a flu-like illness was that not only was my body still producing too little hormone, the numbers were excessive. My health was very much in jeopardy and it was time to take the hormone replacement prescribed by my doctor.

This time of feeling so unwell, this experience of listening to my deep voice of wisdom was unlike any other for me. I didn't focus on expression or balancing my chakra, I didn't eat a gluten free or vegan diet, I didn't call friends for healing sessions. I didn't try to force away the feelings of devastation, depression, and failure. I simply listened to myself, honored what I felt in my body and could sense was true, and began the path of healing — my path of healing.

I share this story with you because there are no specifications for how the Divine Feminine shows up in our lives. There is no law or rule or guidebook to follow so you know you've done the right thing. The truth of what is "right" for each of us comes in the moment of listening, of honoring, of releasing and surrendering into our own intimate truth.

We are the masters of our lives. Too easily we forget this reality, releasing the reins to old-founded beliefs and expectations. Our greatest power lies in turning inward, in allowing ourselves to hear what is real and true from within rather than trying to find what it is we'd like to hear, what is acceptable and even celebrated in our circles.

There are few who understand, allow, and

honor the gifts of illness. There are many who judge and feel there must be something an individual isn't doing or is missing or has done to cause their illness—something to be fixed. I've been guilty of this very thing, and my own illness this time around has brought to me a compassion for myself, and for others.

Perhaps the greatest gift contained in this time of feeling unwell for me was been the embrace of what feels "dark." Some call it the Dark Feminine. She brings with her a sense of loss, of loneliness, of emptiness and unknowing. This aspect of the Feminine is very unlike the fiery, sensual side of her I feel within myself. This dark womb is much more melancholy, and carries with her a very different form of internal surrender and unraveling.

Return to the Holy Womb

There remains within each of us a knowing that we are moving through an experience that is for us, working in our favor, drawing us ever closer to what is sacred in us and those we love. The knowing is there, and still the emotional waves come with a near vengeance, relentless. Initially, we may forget how much we crave the darkness, the womb space, the comfort of feminine presence and grace, the release that comes with every tear that falls.

A majority of my time for nearly two months was spent resting—two weeks straight of lying on the couch. All the while, my world was changing rapidly. I made changes to my life that seemed without reason to others—and in truth, I wasn't always aware of the reasoning myself. Only the reality was crystal clear. The choices were laid out for me in black and white; the purpose was very gray. I couldn't even fully connect to it, nor—thankfully—did I have the energy to try. I simply surrendered into my illness, and gave myself to her completely.

What I have discovered as a result is a more intimate space with my self. I'm certain I cried tears that had been living in me for some time— not because I avoided crying before, but because this time, this space, this illness were all created by me, for me, to sink deeper into me, to feel the sensation of loneliness, to walk alone and in the darkness. This was my time, my experience. I was too tired to make it pretty or nice, to try to find explanations that would work for everyone else.

This darkness is a natural part of who we are. We come from darkness, living in the womb of our mothers for nearly 10 months before making our way into the light. We are happy, secure, cared for, loved, rocked, cradled, appreciated, anticipated, and celebrated while in the womb—

most of us. We thrive and grow and mature in that space. We aren't questioning why there is no light, we aren't mutating ourselves just to please someone else—we simply ARE.

This time of illness was my return to the womb. I had literally just finished the book *Womb Wisdom*, a book I loved in which the authors, Padma and Anaiya Aon Prakasha, spoke of clearing our womb, reclaiming it as our own, even returning to that space of time in our mother's womb to understand more of who we are. I recognize now as I sit here and share with you that that's exactly what I did during my dark time.

In reading the book, there was a knowing it was happening. It was the kind of book that you not only read but experience and feel happening to you without any effort of your own. I didn't bother to do most of the exercises at the end of each chapter. I read them and moved on. My body, my own Divine Feminine presence and knowing guided me right to where I needed to be.

She lives in the darkness. She is there, waiting for us. Her way is not to magically take away the ripples and waves of emotion we feel, but to sit with us, kiss our forehead, perhaps rocking us as we weep and cry and sometimes even complain. She allows us to say we are frustrated and tired and unaware of which end is up or down. She showers grace over us gently, quietly. She moves us in the way our souls call us to go. She hears the whispers we are not yet attuned to, the tender nudges calling out through our own heartsong. This is the Divine Feminine, the Dark Feminine. She is Us. We are Her.

Beauty in the Unbecoming

She comes in as a gentle hush, settling herself ever deeper into our being, drawing upon the ancient strands of feminine magic and wisdom. There is a pulse of all life being awakened in each one of us. We are holy carriers of the Divine Feminine, and she is here, now, whispering into the recesses of our sacred hearts.

Only, we're not fully accustomed to her ways, and from years—lifetimes—of patriarchal programming, we have grown to neglect and fear her. What I love most in the writing and sharing of this book is our willingness to tap into her power and become fully and deeply awakened.

Time has seen her silenced, suffocated, hidden away. Her darkness has become translated as evil, promiscuous, weak, and foolish. We've turned upon ourselves, stepping out of balance with our own natural rhythm. We have forgotten who we are—and now is our time of both remembering and embodying.

There is a beauty in the process of unbecoming, a beauty with which we are quite unfamiliar. The experience of our heart breaking open by the sheer force of the love we are has been lost to us. With each crack and every searing, we draw more fully into our selves through the art of our allowing.

The Sacred Heart knows the force of love intimately. She understands the mystical power of its presence, the tsunami-like disruption of chaotic holy love stirred in its wake. She allows the rupture, bleeding and cracking to undo her, reordering her life and all she has known to this point — over and over again.

She gives herself fully to the divine grace pressing its way through blood and bones, tearing at the very membrane and fiber of her being. For the Sacred Heart — the Divine Feminine — there is an ecstatic rapture in the embrace of this piercing love.

For thousands of years we have feared its penetration, shuttering ourselves away from the heartache of baring our true power.

As women, we have effectively "closed our legs" to all we are and all we have been since the beginning of time. Our men both dampen their ability to penetrate as well as idolize it. The secrecy of a lover's heart has forced its pulsing to become deeply buried in corners of darkness, shrouded in fear.

I offer to you that our very essence, the purest form of all we are, lies nestled there, in the heart shadows. We hide from its power—the power of undoing. There is a tremendous force waiting yet to be released, uncontained from every dark crevice of our being. It lives in our hearts, our wombs, our sex. We've locked it up tight, nearly swallowing the key in the haste to escape our selves.

As a result, there are significant impacts upon our Divine Feminine expression, for both men and women. Women have rejected the feminine in favor of masculinity and equality. Men tone down or feverishly become heightened in their own masculinity in turn. Sexuality lurks in the shadows rather than breathes its beauty in the light of day. The heart is put on hold, creating a zombie-like, mechanistic way of being, driven toward a superficial mode of success and happiness.

We have needed the decades of movement toward equality for women in the physical world. The unfortunate side effect has been a loss of our innate feminine gifts. We are nurturers, caretakers, mothers, wise women, healers, and lovers by our tender and fierce nature. The quest for equality has left us hardened—a hardening against ourselves. In our desire for balance, we've unconsciously asked and expected the same of our men.

As women, we have striven to prove we are worthy of equality in a "man's world." In order to do so, we willingly surrender our feminine way of being and take on in full force the masculine traits already present within us, only in amplified fashion. The impact has been gloriously liberating, historically profound, and soul shattering all at once.

Existing in a world where we impose our own order onto things, life, patterns, and relationships—we understand there is a natural movement at work, even when energies feel and are out of balance. We don't observe here out of a need to "fix," only from the desire to surrender into what is revealing itself to us. I believe the Divine Feminine offers to each of us, male and female alike, a space through which to enter into holy, intimate union with the sacred in ourselves and each other.

Sacred Heart: Portal to Ecstasy

The heart as center point of our truth, passion, undoing, and becoming is our greatest doorway. Close your eyes a moment and breathe through your heart with full intention to simply feel you. Set expectations aside and just feel, trusting whatever you do—or don't—experience. Sink into yourself with an understanding that whatever is alive and at work in your being becomes infused with divine power when you allow your heart to feel your attention. A softening occurs, dissolving away old, dead layers of what is no longer yours or true, while at the same time creating space for the concentrated juice of all you truly are and feel to be expressed through your bodies in powerful ways. Love becomes intensified, sharpened, clear, and unburdened by guilt, fear, or expectations of others. Your interior world is reordered, and some expression of your self forever altered. This, the pure holiness of your Divine Feminine, awaits you here, through the portal of your Sacred Heart.

For the men in our lives, the impact of neglecting the Divine Feminine suffers an equally suppressing state—hardening, making small, bearing immense weight of guilt, causing disfiguration of the sacred, natural form and expression of masculine energy. The sheer power of authentic masculine presence has become distorted, both literally and figuratively.

Let us pause here and very directly and clearly allow for both men and women to welcome every response to these words. Our world more and more evolves into a place where the lines of gender and sex become blurred, and the heart's true form takes the lead. Allow yourself to feel all you do as you move through these pages, without judgment or rejection of what arises, of who you truly are.

The masculine in its true form is hungry to be felt, very much as is the feminine. The art of allowing, receiving, surrendering into the penetration is held by the feminine. Her masculine counterpart can often drive the process. There is a force in the masculine energy that is and feels very different than feminine power. Often the masculine is connected to movement, taking action, acting upon what is felt in the pure heart. In the quieting of that inner voice—the distancing of ourselves from the Divine Feminine—we are actively shutting away the masculine at the same time. Although the false, surface masculine may appear to be full throttle, creating an imbalance that is seemingly masculine over feminine, it in truth can be broken down into self rejection. They dance even in the space of rejection, if somewhat awkwardly.

Men and women alike are hungry for the nectar of the heart's pure love. We long to feel its depth, to become fully penetrated by its searing presence, utterly engulfed in the ecstasy we subconsciously remember it holds for us. We ache for the intensity that comes with the breaking open of our sacred heart.

In quieting the heart, we silence the masculine in our men, asking them to be less than they are, to express and hold their power in a way that doesn't trigger or threaten our hardened survival. The time of woman (feminine) as victim and man (masculine) as aggressor has run its course. We must come to terms with our own true masculine/feminine, each one of us. Entrance into that space can be found through the heart — raw, vulnerable. We forget the massive strength present in the practice of surrender.

The Holy Penetration

In connection to our own self-betrayal is the suppression of our own sexuality. We relate it to a loss of control, manipulation, violation, sin — so many trigger words attached to our sexuality. In our rejection of our selves, of our ability to feel, to connect, to arouse and respond, we've neglected and forgotten the nuance and power of intimacy.

Intimacy with our selves demands acceptance, and indeed a cherishing and honoring of our own sexual nature as part of all we are. Because so much of what we feel has become taboo, secret, hidden, uncomfortable, we've become disconnected and disembodied from ourselves and each other.

Sexuality and creation are one and the same. One fuels the other. Consider the process of creating — we are "making alive," breathing life into, awakening, birthing. The beautiful art of our sexual connection bears the same energetic frequency. Through intimacy with our bodies we are breathing life into all we are. This covers so much: relationship to our physical body, embrace of our emotional body, tuning into our spiritual knowing, and connecting deeply with another on any level. All of this is delicately and powerfully turned on with our sexual presence, expression, and pleasure.

Here we circle back to the Heart — the practice and grace of embracing and celebrating all we are. It's the dark corners and crevices that hold our most treasured self. What we tend to judge or feel judged as ugly, unacceptable, and wrong is the very space longing to feel the power of our gentle focus and surrender. We often find the purest essence of who we are in the most tender and protected terrain of the heart, for it is here the Divine Feminine pulses with wild life, cloaked in darkness, awaiting us in the shadows with her arms spread wide. In Her fullness she sacredly kisses our nakedness, melting away the shame and guilt harbored in our psyche for lifetimes.

The Heart is calling us all now — our own hearts as well as the universal and global heart. We are learning to beat in time with the rhythm of our Mother — as both Mother Earth because we are citizens of her planet, and the Divine Mother who has birthed and holds us all in her love.

There is a beautiful peace in that knowing, in our willingness to feel it—divinely held in her arms, aroused by the flames of all we are as Her.

Imagine yourself leaning back into her. It matters not if you are male or female. Close your eyes and give yourself to her, knowing, trusting fully that she is there to embrace you with all she is—with lifetimes of loving and knowing you intimately. This is a force of holy love offered to us through the Divine Feminine—one we are empowered to offer to all whom we touch in every way. In truly allowing ourselves to enter this sacred space, we can easily feel overcome with the sheer ferocity of holy love. The "work" is not easy, but it is simple. It requires a continual coming back into her, which is a potent coming back into our unique and sacred selves.

If we truly wish to become opened into all she gifts us, we have only to say yes and experience the magic that unfolds. Her nature is such that needs no prompting, practicing, or agonizing. She moves with the mysteries, as a holy mystical force carried deep within the Sacred Heart.

She waits there for us...

Possessed of the very same hungered longing to feel our presence as we hold to feel hers...

We have only to say yes.

JACQUELINE L. ROBINSON is a fiery visionary of the heart. She has recently come to understand her intense soul desire to lead others in reclaiming their own voice, body, love, and sexual nature as the Sacred Feminine. She shares her heart and passion through her writing, and is presently in the process of creating her first book.

Sacred erotic awakening is the current calling in her life, and she follows the intimate voice of her heart in understanding each "next step."

Jacqueline has studied mysticism with Andrew Harvey and Caroline Myss, attended mystery school at Chartres Cathedral in France, as well as taken an intensive course in mediumship with medium Lisa Williams. In 2012, she began creating private women's retreats and virtual groups to break through the patriarchal barriers and integrate an expansive, holy, and sensual way of being.

A New England native, Jacqueline now savors life in Atlanta with her husband and three grown children.

She can be found on her website at **JackieLRobinson.com**, on Facebook at **Facebook.com/KissingtheSacred**, and on Twitter at **@KissingSacred**. Email Jacqueline at **Jackie@JackieLRobinson.com**

BRITTANY N. SELLE

A Call to Awakening

I SPENT MY YEARS running from The Goddess, choking back Her words and Her tears. I ran from Her because, at the time, it seemed easier than owning up to Her power, and therefore to mine.

Owning up meant breaking down and standing exposed in the presence of those who would stone me for what glimmer of divinity inside myself threatened the sensitive balance of their belief structure. I lived in a dark closet because when I had dared to shine before, the light inside of me was snuffed out coldly, and I was told to be grateful for it.

I was being taught how to meld into a society framework that supports the status quo and undermines the individuality in each person. The real hypocrisy is that while society considers it their duty to keep people within the boundaries of safe expression, our individual longing to claim our truth is seen in how we idolize those who have dared step outside of the box and succeeded.

Acting as a beacon to the masses, these idols attempt to call us into our own power, yet they shine so brightly on the throne created for them, and we are blinded. We want to believe we are capable of shining too, but it is easier to watch another do it, and in comparison, we only feel dimmer. It is easier than standing exposed in our own power, and therefore daring to be vulnerable and let down our walls.

These idols represent the secret desires in every woman's heart. It is here they live and feed and form an untouchable model that we compare ourselves to, and when we are unable to meet the unreachable mark, we turn the light within us down to a faint, and flickering flame.

We so deeply yearn for the courage to emulate the confidence these "special" women wear, but our fears have bound us. We want to be worshiped for our beauty, a beauty that is deeper than the skin, a beauty that is mirrored in the regeneration of the womb space. Imagine the freedom in a death and rebirth laid open for all to see—shameless and honest and real. Imagine the freedom in being exactly who we are—no standards to meet or expectations to live up to. Imagine a freedom so great that we may express the depth of our emotion fearlessly and allow it to transform us AND the world!

But the glittering idols we fashion ourselves after are so often hollow, leaving us emptier than we were before, a rattling skeleton with no flesh to relate to.

We take these hopes, based in falsehood, and we wear them like masks. We give them symbolic attachments, and we associate beauty with certain signs and symbols. We created an impossible model, and we did it on purpose. There is something easier in admitting we will never fit a standard, than daring to make our own mold. There is something easier about matching a formula than attempting to solve our own unique equation—and we fall victim to self-created and imprisoning patterns every moment we dim our inner light for the comfort of others.

How can we be expected to shine, Sisters, when this is how we have been taught to view the world? How can we teach our sons and daughters to respect this nameless thing that has been stripped from us?

Our emotions may be seen like a reckless river, tearing apart the structures built with reason and intent, but just as this power within us has grown unfocused and wild, so it can be tamed and channeled into something far greater than ourselves.

Should we find a way to marry this unfathomable power to our identity as women, we will become an impenetrable force that awakens the power in everything we touch.

Will we take that emotion, like an ocean in our belly, and channel it into rebuilding our daughters, so they stand strong like mountains? Do we have the power within us to embrace the cycle of death and rebirth we live each month, and release, with our dying womb, the dogma and programming instilled in us since Eve's rebellion?

Too often I witness women and girls stuffing their truth away, and they do it because they have been taught to. I watch as these women shrink inside of themselves until they no longer know who they are, and they believe the lies they have been fed. To the mothers and wives, the daughters and sisters, the needs of others always come first, and I'm here to tell you *give yourself the love YOU need now*, because there will come a time when your soul will demand it.

I watch as my Sisters grow ill and depleted. I watch as breast cancer and depression, eating disorders and addictions grow and devour us, and I refuse to stand idly by to witness it one moment longer! These illnesses arise out of an imbalance within ourselves. We give and give and give of ourselves, and we repress our own needs until our body mirrors our soul's suffering. But the beauty we search for is always around us. Even as a grain of sand—irritating and abrasive—may eventually form a pearl, so may our suffering shape us if we allow it.

Our walls must be torn down—the one scenario we fought to avoid all along. If we slow down and look for them, beautiful lessons lie in our path. We are left to discover ourselves through the challenges we are presented with in this life, so that we may grow and learn to understand our true self just a little bit better. Like a river, our illnesses have the power to teach our soul how to run its natural course. May we as women learn from water, that with intention of movement and surrender to the moment, we too have the power to carve a way through seemingly any obstacle in our path, just as the river persistently cuts through walls of stone over the passage of time. This is our power.

It is a dance that involves total surrender to the moment, but like birth and the labor leading up to it, when we stop fighting and fearing the contractions and quaking of the womb, and we ride each wave with conscious attention, the process becomes a beautiful blossoming journey instead of a forceful unraveling. It becomes an act of acknowledging the ways in which we have allowed ourselves to be imprisoned, and with each honest acceptance of truth, we remove one bar from our cage. It is a personal and singular journey, but it is one that can be shared, echoed, and mirrored in each human being's individual cycle of growth.

I came to this life with a gift, and I'm here to tell you, so did you — will you nurture it? This gift is uniquely yours, and it is time to claim it.

Though each of our gifts are different, there is one thing that will always bond us, if we can face the inevitable purge of limiting beliefs built over the lifetime of our souls, and we can face the symbolic death involved in such a purging, we can again find peace in a beautiful regeneration that we were born to demonstrate. We can learn to deconstruct our ideas of ourselves and of life, and tear down any barriers in the way of recognizing our own worth and divine nature.

Our distinct purpose in this life is to recognize the spark of God within ourselves. We are one small piece of all that is, expressing itself in a perfect way. We are not meant to fit a perfect mold, but to stand apart, distinct and different, relating only in the acknowledgment of our shared divinity. If we can learn to sit with ourselves and ache in the solitude, if we can walk into the struggle instead of fight it, if we can embrace that part of ourselves that sets us apart, we are reborn, and life takes on new color and new meaning.

With me, Sisters, release your pain—oftentimes nameless—to the Mother. In her embrace, know your truth. It may start faint, a glimmer drawing you in to examine it. A voice whispering your name on the wind. A fish-hook in your belly pulling you in new directions. An awakening moment. Trust where you are being drawn for truth awaits you.

In the image and power of the Hawaiian volcano Goddess Pele, we may first notice the destructive force of such an awakening. We may bleed for all to witness and stand exposed in ourselves, and feel that discomfort, but in accepting our shadow, it will no longer own us. In facing our fears we will learn our power. And as the red hot magma bursts out of the Mother, and the depths of the ocean embrace her new form, then beautiful, fertile ground is created, and we can now choose the seeds we plant there. We can begin defining ourselves differently, and all it took was surrendering to our natural state of being.

All we must do is invite this process into our lives. May we ask to be realigned in our prayers, and then in our actions. May we ask for each moment to be a rebirth, a shedding of the old paradigms which limit us and would serve to limit our daughters and granddaughters from the truth of their own unique expression? For that is what we are, Sisters: we are the rebirth, and we are regeneration. We are the shedding of the old and embracing of the new. We go to prove that out of all death, a beautiful transformation is possible—so how can we continue to define our worth by these dated standards?

We are ever changing and growing, and the girl we were yesterday is not the woman we are today. Let us not re-open our wounds unless we intend to redress them and heal them wholly with new intention. Let us not poke at our old bruises, or wear our shame like a garment draped over us, allowing it to color our world. Let us feel the feelings, grieve the loss of our youth, our innocence, our power, and then as we are designed to do, release it and prepare to nurture, grow, and create the next version of ourselves for ourselves and for all of humanity.

There are times it comes easier to notice our judgments of others first. It is important that we take note of how we have been shaped, and then realize that each judgment has a root in our own insecurity.

When we begin to do this, we may also observe some things that begin reshaping our view of beauty. Every woman that we cross paths with will be at a different stage of her journey. Sometimes, she will be our teacher, and other times we may be hers, but if we truly wish to nurture and embrace this new growing part of ourselves, then it is vital that we see ourselves as one part of a greater Sisterhood—and a Sisterhood's strength comes from the way in which those who are a part of it support each other.

In tearing down another sister for stepping into her truth, we secretly deliver the blow onto ourselves. We are one in the same, and though our lessons may be different, our bodies, our circumstances, that same flickering light exists within all living beings, and should we want ours to grow and shine, we should want all others to grow and shine also.

We cannot judge another person—not their struggles or their pain—by comparing it to that of anyone else. Pain is pain and courage is courage, and it takes courage to claim our authentic self. Undermining another's journey by implying our suffering is greater does no good. May we rather share the wisdom imparted on us in our own unique journey in a way that lifts others up, helps them embrace their lessons, and shows each person their worth? May we choose love when offered the choice, and notice that pain is not a competition, and that loving another does not mean that we endorse their behaviors or that we agree with their point of view. Love just is. Love is effortless, even if our ego creates all kinds of systems, beliefs, and walls that sometimes distract us from this truth.

My deepest hope is that we as women should learn to give of our body, both life and the energy to sustain it, but also learn to honor ourselves in this process and give, but not to our detriment. May we learn to receive, but not in unhealthy imbalance.

This life is a constant act of finding our center and identifying that which keeps us from remaining there. It's a process of ascension and growth that requires a frequent weeding out of old standards and a strong sense of personal responsibility to be ever striving for a purer expression of our divinity. We must live with compassion and share of ourselves, but do so without taking on the responsibility of another's lessons and path of learning.

It is in living our truth that we give others the strength and courage to live their own. Let us choose love in all situations, both paying tribute to others and in honoring ourselves and our own path. A true path of ascension is marked by our ability to see our own lessons and learning in everything that crosses our path, and so we must acknowledge that each person, especially those who may challenge us, act as our mirror and reflect back that which currently limits us. With this mindset we overcome the Ego, and find a humble student within ourselves. We also find a sacred path of lessened suffering. In our humbleness we can accept that if all things we are presented with are only meant to help us grow and understand our own solitary path and relationship to God, then why waste our time in feelings of anger or worries of being misunderstood?

It is true that we cannot force or convince another to grow or shine if they are not ready, but we may love them and lead by pure example.

And when we stumble on our path, we may choose to hide from it in shame, or claim it and let it shape us. If we witness another who stumbles, will we lift them up or tear them down for our own glory and satisfaction? And so, if we should also stumble, we must get up, refuse to shame ourselves for a vulnerable moment, and show ourselves the same love we would a stranger in a similar position. We have the power to use our lessons as fuel, hurling us forward to face our fears, and helping us to cultivate an unrelenting determination to master this process. It is an ever evolving state of being and the learning never ceases. With this mindset we release expectation of outcome, and allow a greater plan to unfold in our lives. We find the deeper symbolism in all circumstances, and we allow ourselves to be changed by them, affirming our faith as we do so. When we embrace the singular journey, and release our fears of walking our path alone, we find the truth of which connects us.

We are each on a singular journey, and this fact can unite us—even if our beliefs or place in life differ. Our bond is this path to our own awakening, regardless of our differences. Let us embrace this.

And so I plead with my Sisters, be the role model your heart always longed for. Where an idol sits upon a throne and feigns perfection, a role model has fallen before us, and risen like a phoenix from the ashes.

Sisters, she has experienced great pain and has let it transform her like the river current shapes and smoothes the roughest stone. A role model has used their suffering to grow and reach and strive for something more than themselves, and has mapped their pain out for us. They have showed us their darkest moments, and in their vulnerability and humanness, given us permission to be exactly who we are. Like the river rock, smooth and rounded, we can allow the flowing currents of our lessons to shape us.

Will you embrace this pilgrimage to find your center again? Your soul knows the steps to this sacred dance, and your heart knows the rhythm that will lead you there. We are provided this inner compass—and really, we always know the direction we are being called to, even if our fear may temporarily confuse us.

To embrace our gifts means to embrace a path

of learning and growth that requires acknowledgement of our weaknesses while having courage enough to wear them for all to see. When we do this, a sense of relief permeates our being and our life. We realize the walls we have worked so hard to hold up and build up are not needed and only served to comfort others. It becomes easier to identify those influences in our lives that do not support this higher truth and to let go of them. It becomes easier to forgive ourselves for not meeting this impossible standard that has been created for us, and to embrace who we really are fully, with the utmost love.

You are worthy. You are worthy. You are worthy.

I have started this healing for you, and I have cried tears for your wounds. I have cried for the women shamed for the rape of their body or blamed for the birth of a fatherless child. I have shed tears for the painful remarks of others, meant to hold you in your prison. I have wept for the women who keep their truth locked deep inside of their hearts for fear of letting it fall to the hands of those who treat it less than the sacred jewel it is.

My heart has died and been reborn for the women throughout history who have carried these lessons forward for us today, so that we may not suffer like they did. May we honor their progress and their learning, because really, we ARE every woman.

Let us break the bonds placed on womankind through all time until this very moment in history, and write a new story for ourselves and our daughters!

Let me watch you blossom!

Know that for every voice that shoots like arrows into your exposed and blooming heart, there are ten silent songs sung in your honor! For every attempt by another to fit you back into that box you once inhabited, there are thousands of women, past and present, calling you to your truth with fire in their eye! Let us look to real role models, and release our idols from their gilded cages.

In their freedom, we are free, Sisters.

Embrace your Goddess, and walk this Earth with me, renewed.

————————————◦❊◦————————————

BRITTANY N. SELLE is an Intuitive Life Coach, Healer, Artist, Medium, and mother of four from the North Idaho region.

Having had intuitive/psychic sensitivities from childhood, she learned to sharpen her gifts over the last seven years, offering readings and intuitive consultations, teaching workshops and classes, and founding a support group called

Circle of Spirit (now primarily online via Facebook) for those opening to their own gifts.

Brittany is a firm believer that each person born to this world has come with a purpose, and where it is not readily known, we sometimes need help finding our path.

She specializes in helping to identify the meaning and lessons of growth behind certain events or traumas, breaking patterns that span lifetimes, and helping others locate their unique intuitive gifts and life purpose.

For more information on Brittany, and to see what she is up to, check out her website at **GuidedLifeCoaching.com**

BETH SHEKINAH TERRENCE

Igniting Our Hearts and Souls

I DREAM OF A woman running away from a life of pain in a time long, long ago. She runs across the vacant desert, not knowing where she is going, only that she is seeking shelter — not a shelter for her physical body, but one for her soul.

After hours, maybe days of walking, running, crying, and feeling the shame of many lifetimes, she comes upon a small opening to a cave. She crouches down to enter. Tentatively, she pushes her body through the crevice, and rather than feeling fear as she imagines she would, she feels a sense of comfort she has never before known.

This feeling envelops her, and she senses a spark of light emerging. She realizes this spark is not within the darkness of the cave—it lies within her own being.

She begins to hear a voice calling her deeper and deeper into the cave, and deeper and deeper into herself. As she moves, she finds a series of steps, which lead her into a hidden chamber, glistening, as it's lined with gold!

The voice guides her to a small altar at the far end of this cavernous space. She lights an oil lamp, and makes an offering with the few withered flowers she picked from her garden when she left her home and one of the few remaining dates that have been nourishing her on her journey into the unknown. She places these items on the altar, saying a prayer from deep in her heart and asking for this glimpse of comfort that has begun to envelope her to guide her forward.

As she stands and makes her offering, the chamber begins to glisten with little sparks of light, just like the one she was beginning to sense deep within her own heart and soul. The voice she has heard begins to sing a song. It gets louder and stronger. She can begin to make out the words: *"Inanna*, Inanna He, Inanna, Inanna He"*

As she hears these words—which her mind doesn't recognize—she knows in a deep way that she is home. She feels a sense of safety and love wash over her, something she has never known!

She lays down upon the ground, which is soft and feels like it is cradling her, as her mother once did long ago. She rests there for how long she cannot tell, but as she does, she receives what she later will come to know as an initiation.

That day, in the depths of that cave and the glistening light of this sacred space, this wandering woman awoke to the Sacred Feminine inside of her. She connected with the goddess she came to know as Inanna and many others. She knew she was being asked to carry the spark of light that was now burning brightly in her heart and soul through the dark times to come. It was clear to her that a masculine energy had begun to take over the reigns of the world—she realized now that was why she had been running.

She was told that a time would come when the Sacred Feminine would be reawakened in the heart and souls of all beings, but even when it was not, it would always be there nurturing, supporting, and loving the children of the earth. She sat in the cave for forty days and forty nights; she saw times past, and times future. She saw that cycles of energy happen, and that this is the nature of creation. She understood that this pulling back of the sacred feminine was not due to weakness or victimization, but was a part of the divine story.

Contraction/Expansion
Ebb/Flow
Decay/Growth
Death/Life
All are One!

Later she invited other women to join her in the cave. She taught them what was revealed to her. They came to the cave to remember. They came together to celebrate, to sing and to dance — to honor the divine essence within them.

A time came when death reigned on the city where the women came from and they could no longer return to this sacred place. The cave was forgotten, but the spark that was ignited there was carried forward in each woman's hearts and souls.

* * * * * * *

In another time and place...

Friday was a busy day in the village. Lots of preparation needed to happen before the Sabbath came. Food to be gathered, prepared, and cooked. Cleaning to be done. Work to be finished before the weekly day of rest was to begin.

If one could contrast this hectic busyness of one day with the quiet stillness of the next, one might know the Shabbat Kallah* — the Sabbath

Bride—had come. How else could you explain this shift?

You might say each man and each woman had chosen to shift in this way, each week, as it was commanded in the Torah*. But could they really make this powerful of a shift on their own? Was it by following the outer laws so strictly that its transformation arose, or was it a divine romance awakened in the heart and soul of each person as the Sabbath Bride arrived each week?

As the veil of the Shabbat Kallah (bride) descended upon them, this shift was effortless. It was as if the real, mundane world of everyday life disappeared, and this little village in Eastern Europe stepped into the mystery, into the divine.

In the Zohar*, a Jewish spiritual and mystical text, it is said of the Sabbath that "One must prepare a comfortable seat with several cushions and embroidered covers, from all that is found in the house, like one who prepares a canopy for a bride. For the Shechinah* is a queen and a bride. This is why the masters used to go out on the eve of Sabbath to receive her on the road, and used to say: 'Come, O bride, come, O bride!' And one must sing and rejoice at the table in her honor... one must receive the Lady with many lighted candles, many enjoyments, beautiful clothes, and a house embellished with many fine appointments..."

* * * * * * *

As a child, I'd often spend the Sabbath with my grandparents, who had come from that village in Eastern Europe. They carried this light with them to their modern apartment in New York City. As we gathered there in "Queens," things seemed in some ways to be the same as in the village. Fridays were a day of busily preparing. My grandfather would rush to finish work early. My Grandmother would shop, cook, and prepare the house for the Sabbath Bride.

As sunset approached, my Grandfather would hurry off to the synagogue to pray Mincha and Maariv—the afternoon and evening prayers to be said immediately before and after sunset.

Once the preparation was done, my Grandmother and I would set the table and get out the candle sticks that she was given as a wedding gift in that village in Eastern Europe— those very same candlesticks that welcomed the Shabbat Kallah in a land so far away.

Lighting the Sabbath candles is a ritual that is practiced in the Jewish tradition by women only. Often people look at Judaism and other Judeo-Christian religions as solely patriarchal, and in many ways they are. However, there are some sacred practices that show the special place that women hold in this tradition. One might say that women were not welcome in the synagogue to pray, but actually, they were staying home to be the ones to welcome the divine mystery into their lives and their home.

Lighting the candles seems so simple. Two candles, a blessing, a ritual that symbolizes the return of the light.

We light the candles, we cover our eyes. We say the blessing, we move our hands over our heads three times to welcome the Shabbat Kallah—the bride, the light, the Shechinah.

It is in standing in this light and invoking the Sacred Feminine that we transform from the energy of the everyday into that of the divine mystery. It is through this same sacred vessel— not of body, but of spirit—that we came to this earth, and it is where we will return to when we die.

As we observe the Sabbath, each week the Bride comes to visit us, to remind us of who we are. As we rest and sit in stillness, we know our essence. We're reminded of the bigger picture of life. This is the power of the Sacred Feminine. We can do this in many ways—as we sing, as we dance, as we pray—we ignite that spark that was found in the cave so very long ago. What then seemed to be an outer cave, we now know is actually the pathway to a return to wholeness and to our soul.

* * * * * * *

It has been many years since my beloved Grandma Clara passed away. And, my weekly practice of lighting the Sabbath candles has gone, too. There are many who continue this practice today in the Jewish tradition, or many others who honor the Sacred Feminine in different ways, in other religions and traditions. Yet, even those who practice these rituals may not remember the deepest essence of the practices and what they invoke. It seems like in our modern world there is a powerful disconnect, which keeps us from connecting with the essence of the Sacred Feminine. We live in a world that is masculine in so many ways.

In the Jewish mystical teachings, the world is seen as broken and shattered — it's on its way to being mended. There is a sense of being in Exile that presents itself in a variety of ways. It is said that part of the world's brokenness stems from the withdrawal of God when the Shechinah, the Divine Feminine aspect, was exiled from its proper place in the world. The Sabbath Bride and the rest she brings is seen as a gateway to our reconnection with this essence, and offers a return to wholeness.

This metaphor of the separation, which was to have occurred between the masculine aspect and the feminine aspect of the God — the estrangement of the "King" from the "Queen" — is one that is shared in many spiritual traditions of the world.

It is said that as the Shechinah returns to this world, she seeks out our most precious sparks, and rescues them from the shells of darkness they have been hidden in for so long. It is in this reconnection that we find meaning and sacredness in our lives.

Today, there is much discussion about a return to the Sacred Feminine. But is there really a return happening? And, even in saying this, what do we truly know about what it means to marry the Sacred Feminine and Sacred Masculine in our lives and our world? Are we going through the motions of practices, rituals, and reciting prayers, or are we actually invoking, embracing, and embodying this Great Mystery in our lives?

There was a time when we needed to have a day of the week, a Sabbath, to remind us of this and to reawaken to the truth of who we are. Now, in the incredible chaos of our modern world, maybe more than one day a week is needed — we need to awaken each and every day! We need to invite the Shechinah, the Shabbat Kallah, Inanna, or whatever we choose to call the Sacred Feminine, into our lives in a more powerful way. It is entering into this gateway that our caring, compassion, and connection — the energies that can shift and change our world — emerge.

A key part of this lies in having compassion for ourselves, and being willing to create the space to connect with our own deepest essence — our light and our darkness.

It may seem like a ritual or religion is what is needed, and certainly our practices are of benefit, but what is truly needed is for us to enter into the cave that lies within our own heart and soul, to find our inner spark. It is there that we can ignite this spark we have been carrying since the beginning of time.

Are you ready? The time is now!

* * * * * * *

Glossary of Terms:

Inanna - Inanna is the ancient Sumerian goddess of love, procreation, and war who later became identified with the Akkadian goddess Ishtar, and further with the Phoenician Astarte and the Greek Aphrodite, among others. She was also seen as the bright star of the morning and evening, Venus. Inanna was carefully identified with Ishtar, and rose in prominence from a local vegetative deity of the Sumerian people to the Queen of Heaven, and the most popular goddess in all of Mesopotamia.

Shabbat Kallah - meaning "Sabbath Bride." The

Jewish Sabbath is often referred to as the Shabbat Kallah, the Sabbath bride, or *Shabbat Ha Malkah*, the Sabbath Queen. The theme of Shabbat as bride is found throughout the traditional Friday night prayers, which welcomes and honors the sacred energy that comes with her arrival each week.

Shechinah - Shechinah means "to dwell within," and is described as the Divine Feminine aspect of God.

Torah - The Torah or Jewish Written Law, consists of the five books of the Hebrew Bible known as the Old Testament. It is said these books were given by God to Moses on Mount Sinai, and include within them all of the biblical laws of Judaism.

Zohar - Revealed more than 2,000 years ago, the Zohar is a spiritual text composed by Kabbalist Rav Shimon bar Yochai. It consists of twenty-three mystical books that illuminate the secrets of the Bible, the Universe, and many aspects of life.

BETH SHEKINAH TERRENCE is a trained Shaman, Holistic Health & Wellness Practitioner, Speaker, Writer, and Recovery Coach. She has been working in the field of Holistic Healing and Transformation for over twenty years.

Her overall mission is to support others in living a heart-centered, balanced, and joyful life through discovering the healer within. She believes that her own life experience and healing journey has served as a catalyst for the message she brings to the world — that at our core, we are all beings of love, light, and peace. We just need to "remember."

Writing has always been one of Beth's greatest passions. Since childhood, she has written poetry, kept a journal, and written stories. She has several published stories and poems, and she is currently working on a memoir about her healing journey through trauma, which led to the emergence of her soul purpose as a shaman.

Beth's blog, *The Heart Of Awakening: Searching For A New Paradigm*, offers an online resource for transformation and healing. She is also an author, facilitator, and program developer for *Heal My Voice*, a non-profit organization whose mission is to empower and support women and girls globally to heal, reclaim their voices, and step into great leadership in their lives and the world.

To learn more about Beth's writings, healing sessions, or online programs, visit

BethTerrence.com or
TheHeartofAwakening.wordpress.com.

Also, you may find Beth on Twitter **@BethTerrence**.

MELISSA RAE THOMPSON

I HAVE COME A distance from there to here. There being before the change. Here, after the change.

I am still changing, though, because that is an inevitable result of existing here.

Transformation seems the stuff of butterflies. With bright paper wings they flutter until dust. Wind batting these winged flowers until they light or fall down to darkness.

My five-year-old daughter was delighted today. She confided her wish upon a star. She wanted people to do what she wanted them to do.

"The wish did not come true," she said, shrugging. She reflected that it was not the job of stars to grant such power. "I guess this is why my wish did not come true."

I asked her, "What do you wish others would do?"

"Be nice. Play with me. Not be mean to each other."

I agreed that I wished that for her, too. Not on stars, but in my heart. "But we cannot make someone do something. If they do not do it from their heart, then they did not really want to do it. Probably they will not do it again, either, unless someone is watching."

Curiously, she looked up into my eyes. "Does it matter if people are watching?"

"It shouldn't," I admit, "But sometimes people only do things if they think others will see. If others see, they think people will give them high fives, praise, or dollar bills."

Smiling, I take her hand gently into mine, and pull her onto my lap. I see the moon outside the window of our study. Firelight from our fireplace reflects in her eyes.

She snuggles closer, "Mommy, I like high fives and money too."

I tuck an escaped curl behind her ear, "Yes. Me too. I think we all do. If that is the only reason I am a good friend or I do something nice for a stranger though... I am not doing it from my heart."

"Where are you doing it from then?" she asks

me, scrunching up her nose.

"From our minds. When we think too much about things, we are not feeling enough about them."

She is little. In a way she understands what I mean, but there are many, much older, who still do not understand how to balance their hearts with their minds.

The star knew eons before that my daughter made this wish. That she would scrunch up her nose, and with wide eyes, make her wish.

In a way, the star waited for her. Staying lit, even in death, to guide her.

For the wishers and the dreamers, the stars still shine.

By the time she wished upon it, the star had already burned out. What a patient, ancient star to be so patient with a child. This star guide gave her enough time to realize the value of a wish.

Really, compared to the stars, we are all small children. I am her mother, and I make wishes too. I used to sing her a lullaby about stars — stars that were bright enough to hang wishes upon their lighted points.

I wished for a husband that would love me without condition.

I wished for children that would love to learn, and learn to love.

Becoming a mother and wife has been a progression, one that has changed me completely, and only to completely be changed again and again.

I have paid tears to the dirt. Many times. More times than I can count.

There have been times when my struggles were so great, and my obstacles were so fierce that I wondered if I would survive the avalanche, and if I survived that, the resulting wounds.

Life goes on.

We choose to go on, or we choose to stop.

When I look up at the stars though, I realize the stars are patient enough to stay lit for us. Like a parent, stars know it will take time for us humans to catch up.

———————————•ૡ✹ૠ•———————————

MELISSA RAE THOMPSON is wife to Lloyd Matthew Thompson, a mother of four energetic children, and nurturer of two feline fur babies.

Presently, she works at home. She is passionate about mental health, and has a Master's degree in Counseling, Psychology. Melissa is also very interested in physical health, and holds a degree in Medical Massage Therapy.

Being a creative sort, she spends a lot of time with her family enjoying the Arts. Spirituality is very important to her, and she encompasses this in they way she thinks and moves in the world.

STARFIELD
PRESS
Oklahoma City, OK

OTHER TITLES FROM *STARFIELD PRESS*

THE AQUARIAN EMPATH
THE AQUARIAN EMPATH, PART II
THE AQUARIAN HEALER
THE AQUARIAN PATH TO ABUNDANCE
COSMIC LOVE

THE NATURAL HEALER'S GUIDE
LIGHTWORKER: A CALL TO AUTHENTICITY
ENERGYWORKER: A CALL TO EMPOWERMENT
THE HEALER: A NOVEL
AURA: A SHORT STORY

IF GOD WAS A WOMAN

A SUM OF FLAWS: A NOVEL

SOUL STUDIES: ETYMOLOGY AND STORY

ALCHEMY 365: A SELF-AWARENESS WORKBOOK

Find them all at:
www.**StarfieldPress**.com